"Owning our story and loving ourselves through that process is the bravest thing we'll ever do."

—Brené Brown

This book and the spaces depicted within it would not be possible without the courage and vision of our clients who have entrusted us with helping them tell their stories in the pursuit of creating a home that is uniquely their own. It is with profound gratitude that I am able to share them with you.

HOUSES
ROBERT A.M. STERN ARCHITECTS
Cartier
PANTHÈRE

TAILORED INTERIORS

The Bespoke Designs of Patrick Sutton

Written by Vicky Lowry

Foreword by Steele Marcoux

FABRICUT
DIS9008 MOCCASIN
GARRETT
OMO
HARTMANN

Contents

Foreword

Steele Marcoux

"We craft spaces shaped by stories—stories born of dreams and fueled by emotions." This is how designer Patrick Sutton describes the work of his firm based in Baltimore, Maryland, and Palm Beach, Florida. For more than thirty years, Patrick has created award-winning residential and hospitality spaces around the world, including the Sagamore Pendry in Baltimore, recently named one of the top hotels in the country in *Condé Nast Traveler*'s Readers' Choice Awards. Yet Patrick views himself, first and foremost, as a storyteller.

The designer believes deeply that each room that holds us tells a story of who we are and the life we aspire to live. Unlike other designers who develop a certain aesthetic for which they become known and sought after, Patrick comes to each project in search of a story to tell: a specific portrayal of client dreams combined with the unique spirit of the project environment. Through intimate conversations with his clients and in-depth research, he distills a unique narrative distinctive to each project, reflecting the confluence of the project place and personality. The results are authentic interiors that speak volumes about the clients and only a whisper of Patrick's skilled guiding hand.

Perhaps it's no surprise that Patrick has drawn upon his own personal narrative to develop his approach. As a child, he spent years tagging along with his travel-journalist father, Horace Sutton, touring the world's most beautiful places and observing a storyteller at work along the way. When you speak to Patrick, his experience with his father comes up early and often. "My father taught me to see the world as a magical place filled with beauty and adventure waiting to be discovered," he says.

There's no doubt the curiosity instilled in him by traveling with his father has shaped Patrick into the world-renowned designer he is today. And you can see it in the projects featured here, in his second book, *Tailored Interiors*—from an art-filled historic renovation in Washington, D.C., to a new-build private temple of wellness and well-being in Maryland.

I hope you'll find, as I have, these stories about life, dreams, personal history, and environment beautiful and inspiring. And, if you're lucky, you'll find someone like Patrick to help you write your own story into your future.

Jackson Hole Residence
Patrick Sutton
Primary Bedroom
Armoire
Samuel & Sons
Lakeside Lounge
Beach Residence

Introduction

Patrick Sutton's emotional education and psychological examination of his life are as integral to the success of his practice as his training in architecture and decades-long experience as an interior designer. Time and again, Patrick's clients emphasize his gift for listening, for "getting" them, his approachability, and his intuitive instincts. He understood one homeowner's tastes so well, she joked to him, "Get out of my head!" These talents, however, were hard-earned.

On paper, as in his collection of vintage photographs that portray a smiling, impeccably dressed family, Patrick's childhood appeared ideal. His charismatic mother was a fashion model and an actress. His chivalric father, a U.S. Army captain during World War II, swept the former beauty queen off her feet and went on to become a celebrated travel journalist. The family traveled around the world in first-class cabins and stayed in the finest hotels. Patrick's early exposure to such exquisite luxuries surely ignited his curiosity about and passion for design. And yet, behind the glamourous facade, all that glittered was not gold.

Soon after the young family moved to Hawaii, where Patrick's father launched a magazine, his mother began to show signs of schizophrenia. She was just twenty-six years old. As her mental health rapidly deteriorated, Patrick's father buried himself in his work, rarely coming home. Patrick's seemingly picture-perfect childhood became marred by trauma, shame, and loneliness. This was hardly a home where he could invite friends over. But while his schoolwork plummeted, his empathy and emotional intelligence soared. "In order to survive a home absent of role-model parenting, I became a fast student of everyone else, in search of what normal behavior looked like. I watched people's expressions and mannerisms intently," he explained.

Design became an intuitive healing tool for young Patrick, when he could not actually heal his mother. "I wished I could help create a home where my father would come back and be restored with happiness," he recalled. "One of my earliest memories involving interior design was transforming our den into a respite for him. I took his lounge chair and moved it to the center of the room, dimmed the lights, arranged a table next to his chair, and placed an Old Fashioned cocktail on it. I cued up the record player and had Bobby Short crooning as my father came home. I wanted him to be healed, and unwittingly I was using design and atmosphere to do it."

The story of his childhood, however, didn't have to be the story of his life. Patrick excelled in a high school drafting course because of his innate talent for seeing things three-dimensionally. In his junior year, a summer program at Harvard University further ignited his interest in the world of design and architecture. Patrick went on to earn a bachelor's degree in architecture from Carnegie Mellon University, and for a decade held positions at architectural firms in and around Baltimore.

Incorporating interior design into his architectural practice evolved naturally. "I became fascinated with the life that was going on inside the architecture," he explained. "What's a dinner party or raising children going to look like here," he would wonder. In 1994, Patrick launched his eponymous design firm, in downtown Baltimore, and for the past thirty years his compassionate approach to design can be found in the expressive interiors of everything from five-star hotels and stylish restaurants to luxurious homes across the country.

An empath, Patrick has been profoundly influenced by Brené Brown, a research professor at the University of Houston and a prolific author on the subject of embracing one's vulnerability and shame to gain courage and develop sensitivity to others. "My job is to create environments that help my clients to not only realize their dreams and aspirations but to also enhance them to a level they may not have previously considered," Patrick said. "Creating places of wellness and sanctuary—chasing what I could not do for my mother—drives me to design these healing, uplifting environments for those who have entrusted me with their homes."

For a Washington, D.C., couple who recently became empty nesters, Patrick transformed their French country–inspired manse into scintillating contemporary spaces no longer designed for raising children but to embrace a new and energized time in their life. In a new house in the Maryland countryside, he created serene, welcoming interiors to evoke a sense of calm and well-being—an antidote to one family's hard-charging lifestyle. His daring design of another residence in Washington, D.C., features rich saturated colors, distinctive lighting, and wildly imaginative furnishings in a setting that's as ideal for entertaining as it is for relaxing and kicking back.

For a property in Jackson Hole, Wyoming, Patrick declined the typical trappings of the American West for clean lines and a pared-down aesthetic; it's the very definition of a modern take on vacation living. On the Delaware coast, his obsession with details is on full display with brass inlays in the millwork, leather-trimmed walls, and the use of thirty-four different marbles handpicked in an Italian quarry for a newly built retreat with a timeless sensibility and a welcoming vibe for family and friends of every age.

These homes and the others featured in this book portray interiors that are supremely polished but never impersonal. They are eminently livable not only because Patrick infuses his work with emotion, practicality, and warmth but also because of his uncanny ability to envision how his clients should, and will, live in their spaces.

A Passion for Design

WASHINGTON, D.C.

A tech entrepreneur based in Washington, D.C., reached out to Patrick in 2021 to handle the interior design of a residence he had just bought: a charming stone house built in 1926 in a tony, tree-lined neighborhood. The interiors, which had undergone a series of renovations over the last century, had a faded look. The homeowner, a design aesthete who had already built a series of what he called "ultra" houses that excelled at captivating design, put together a new dream team for this project to thoughtfully renovate the property as a unified whole. The ensemble included Patrick Sutton, architect Patrick Cooke of the celebrated firm Thomson & Cooke Architects, and Campion Hruby Landscape Architects. The client gave them all of the means and the freedom to hit the highest notes in creativity.

The goal was to keep intact the beautiful bones of the house, such as its 20-inch-thick stone walls, but to thoroughly gut-renovate the awkward, rabbit-warren layout to create warm yet modern spaces for privacy and entertaining. "This house has stood 100 years and we didn't want to lose or cheapen that," Cooke explained. "The minute we started to explore additions and we proposed more glass, steel, and contemporary details, the homeowner got very excited." The message from the client was clear: "Let's start fresh, let's be adventurous."

New architectural flourishes included an ethereal entrance in a half-moon shape—Patrick calls it "a pause"—that's accented with limestone floors and blackened-steel French doors and windows inset into the thick walls. A sinuous central staircase with delicate railings has a light, graceful presence, and a first-floor rear addition allowed for a light-filled breakfast nook overlooking the gardens and a spacious primary suite. A sculptural plaster staircase that descends to the lower level looks like it's extruded from the earth. "You shed the idea of an old house the minute you walk through the front door," Cooke noted.

Many of the walls were handsomely clad in rift-sawn oak, including those of the dining room, family room, and two small guest bedrooms that have been carved out under the eaves of the top floor—a concept that the homeowner admired in another Washington, D.C., house featured in Patrick's first book. The oak's special finish has the feeling of raw wood—"tactile, approachable, and warm but super refined," according to Patrick.

Virtually every element of the furnishings is distinctive and beguiling, from the artfully designed lighting and the sculptural shapes of the furniture to the judicious use of rich colors like plum, deep green, and blue that infuse the rooms with warmth. In the living room, Patrick juxtaposed green-banded paper sconces that he sourced from the Ralph Pucci design gallery with a gleaming ombré glass–topped cocktail table by glassblower artisan John Pomp.

A tubular alabaster light fixture from the French designer Alain Ellouz floats like a buoy from the ceiling of the family room. "I have clients where everything has to be soft and tactile but with this client it just had to be inspirational," Patrick said. "We could go to some really unique, artful sources and he always picked the coolest thing."

The luscious color scheme was inspired by a striking abstract canvas by mid-century painter Stephen Greene that hangs in the primary bedroom. "That was our story, our talisman," the homeowner said. The artist's saturated hues show up in a guest room's lavender-colored plaster walls, the living room's emerald and prune upholstery, and the dining room's pumpkin-colored chairs below a cobalt-blue geometric sculpture. Meanwhile, a painting by Lucia Lopez in the dining room further informs the color scheme, from a gold-leafed ceiling to a ravishing ruby lacquered console. "That dining room is nuts," the owner admitted. "I was nervous it was going to be too much or not make sense, but it's a delightful room."

Pale blue cabinetry enlivens the primary bath; the powder room has a wall of amethyst-colored marble; and the kitchen holds an eggplant-colored range. "How many clients let you do that," Patrick exclaimed. "Yet nothing is jarring—these are soft, engaging autumnal colors."

"Because my life is crazy with work, I needed a place of serenity," the homeowner said. "Anything that is overwrought is not optimal. On the other hand, the place had to have character and not be too slick. We managed to land it. The house doesn't feel cold, but it is certainly crisp."

BUCCELLATI

BECKER
30 YEARS at
VANITY FAIR
ASSOULINE

Page 12: The foyer of this modernized early-twentieth-century stone house hints at the eclectic spirit within. A rustic hand-carved Mexican chair presides below a 1967 abstract painting by Albert Kotin, while a glass-bauble pendant plays off the garden's greenery.

Previous spread: In the formal living room, an ombré glass–topped brass cocktail table and a bronze-legged armchair shimmer atop a handwoven silk rug, its color pulled from the richly veined Calacatta Viola marble fireplace surround. The green-banded paper sconces are by John Wigmore for Ralph Pucci.

Above: With just a few materials, the spare foyer is a study in simplicity: blackened steel windows and door frames, plaster walls, and honed limestone flooring.

Opposite: Patrick describes the powder room as a "tiny little color bomb." The hand-carved blue quartzite pedestal sink abuts a wall of lavender-veined marble. An organically shaped mirror serves as a whimsical counterpoint to the otherwise linear geometry of the space.

Previous spread: The foyer and dining room beyond abound with eye-catching shapes, from a circular plaster light fixture that appears to grow out of the plaster ceiling to the geometric sculpture that hovers above the dining table to contemporary artworks that electrify the mix. The foyer table displays the homeowner's collection of mudmen figurines.

Above: Cove lighting inserted into the recessed gilded ceiling casts a glamorous glow in the dining room. Patrick chose the colorful sculpture, rather than a chandelier, "because it's more interesting." The custom-made table, crafted in blackened steel with a quartzite top, sits on a woven leather rug.

Opposite: French Deco–inspired brass sconces are a striking element against the rift-sawn oak paneling that envelops the room.

Page 24: Alpaca-and-linen curtains softly filter light and add a luxurious touch in the dining room.

Page 25: The kitchen cabinetry is a handsome mix of bronze-finished steel and dark-stained oak. The island features a fluted base cut from a block of Calacatta marble, while the backsplash is made of Gris de Savoie marble.

Right: With a linen-covered ceiling and textured plaster walls, the beamed family room is a cozy retreat just off the kitchen. The nubby upholstered seating sits atop a chunky hand-knotted rug by Marc Phillips, and Patrick suspended the sculptural alabaster light fixture with leather straps.

wonderland
TAILORING LEGENDS

Page 28: The new wing includes a sunny breakfast nook overlooking the garden and the primary suite beyond.

Page 29: Modern architectural elements, such as the metal roofing and walls of glass and steel, blend harmoniously with the original 1920s stonework.

Opposite: Tactile materials energize the breakfast area, among them hand-finished plaster walls, the banquette's playful woven fabric, and a slubby linen shade on a handmade lamp by plaster artisan Stephen Antonson.

Above: A Calder-like sculpture found on IstDibs hangs above the breakfast table.

Above: A sculptural, rustic plaster staircase makes a bold statement on the lower level, which accesses a mudroom, wine cellar, and recreation room.

Opposite: Streamlined materials—limestone, blackened steel, plaster, and oak—give the lower level a chic, gallery-like look.

Right: Patrick found ample ways to illuminate the recreation room with visual flair. He upholstered the walls with trapezoidal panels that fit together like a puzzle. He found an equally shapely table lamp, and added a punchy contemporary abstract painting.

Following spread: A view from the garden showcases the new addition dedicated to the primary suite.

Sumptuous details, such as mohair upholstery for the custom-made bed and sofa, and softly filtering linen curtains, transform the primary bedroom into a sublime sanctuary. Patrick cut out the center back of the sofa for an even better view of the garden. The moody colors of a mid-century painting by Stephen Greene inspired the palette throughout the house.

ANDY WARHOL
Polaroids 1958–1987
TASCHEN

Left: Patrick designed the oak bedside tables with brass handles, and inserted a patterned Kneedler Fauchère wallcovering into a niche behind the bed. Antique chimes from the homeowner's grandmother hang in the doorway.

Top: A cheerful periwinkle-blue paint was used on the bathroom vanities.

Above: The dressing room features floor-to-ceiling oak paneling.

A new staircase with a delicate steel balustrade and polished walnut steps spirals up three main floors, while a three-tiered handblown-glass chandelier cascades through its core.

Right: In the cozy second-story library flanking two guest bedrooms, Patrick lined the oak paneling with brass inlays—"a subtle but very cool detail," he explained. The niche is covered with a woven grass cloth wallcovering; the color of the bench upholstery came from the painting in the primary bedroom; and the ceiling light fixture by the Urban Electric Company is one of the many alluring lights used throughout the home.

Following spread: Swathing a guest bedroom in different textures using just one hue—in this case a plummy lavender—"is kind of my thing," said Patrick. Matching Venetian plaster walls, a marble fireplace surround, wool drapes, and a woven carpet create a seductively serene environment.

The Art Museum
GLOBAL ARTISANS
MUSIC
THE WAY
Modern
TUSCAN
BEYOND
1,000 PLACES
Lee Radziwill
Robert Ryman
THE WORLD

WISE TREES

Virtually every element of the furnishings is distinctive and beguiling, from the artfully designed lighting and the sculptural shapes of the furniture to the judicious use of rich colors like plum, deep green, and blue that infuse the rooms with warmth.

JOURNEY BY DESIGN

Two small bedrooms are carved out under the eaves of the top floor and clad entirely in cerused oak, including the sculptural windows that recall a yacht's interior. But there's nothing plain about these rooms, as evidenced by a boldly graphic rug and striking lighting.

Above: The spiffy new pool cabana further sheds the idea of this being an old house.

Opposite: Burnished-steel cabinets join a ceiling and walls crafted from planks of cerused oak. The Murano glass pendant light is from the 1960s.

Following spread: The beautifully landscaped grounds and old-growth trees belie the fact that this property is just a couple of miles from downtown D.C.

A Breath of Fresh Air

WASHINGTON, D.C.

The owners of this grand limestone manor in Washington, D.C., were experiencing the classic symptoms of empty nesters when their adult children moved out to start families of their own. They had no interest in downsizing from their finely feathered nest, yet their colorful, Provence-imbued rooms no longer fit their needs or tastes. Instead of interiors that evoked French farmhouse charm, they wanted simplified yet sophisticated spaces, lighter in atmosphere, and with judicious pops of jewel tones—all the better to spotlight their striking collection of artworks.

They found their ideal collaborator in Patrick whose exceptional sense of restraint and mastery of fine details caught their eye. The couple had admired a residence that Patrick had conceived and then perused his website to get a feel for his aesthetic. "The wife told me that she didn't see a single project that she wanted for her own home, but they all looked unique and well done. She told me, 'If he can do that for them, he can do that for me,'" Patrick recalled. So began their four-year journey to shed the feathers of the past and reinvent an airy, crisply tailored home to perfectly suit the way they wanted to live now and into the future.

Patrick's ability to listen carefully and observe keenly served this project well. He discovered early in the design phase that these clients weren't driven by making hurried decisions, but rather by a thoughtful approach with no time limits—a rare luxury in today's fast-paced world. Case in point: Patrick presented some fifty wallcoverings for the new dining room before they settled on an ethereal textured silk. The very first layout he conceived for the spacious living room, which previously featured velvet curtains and floral brocade sofas in autumnal hues, was "a swing and a miss," he admitted. "But by missing, it started a dialogue of what they wanted to achieve that would yield deeply personal results." He rarely made a misstep after that. As the client described, "Patrick got it, he'd hear me. Usually, the first time he made a suggestion was the charm."

After removing the living room's French country details, such as its heavy crown moldings, Patrick bathed the now clean-lined space in shades of lilac, one of his client's favorite colors. By employing different textures in that delicate hue—from the velvet upholstery on a sculptural Vladimir Kagan sofa to the plush silvery rug underfoot and hand-painted ombré finish on the walls and ceiling—Patrick created a glamorous environment with timeless appeal.

He retained the family room's timber beams and antique French fireplace surround but upholstered the walls of the fireplace nook in a cozy dark linen, applied matte Venetian plaster elsewhere, and introduced comfortable contemporary seating, such as a generous sectional sofa and high-back wing chairs. "I like juxtaposing the old and familiar with something new," Patrick explained.

Upstairs in the primary suite, Patrick sought to create "a place of calm, peace, and serenity." Taking cues from the garden below, the designer conjured an elegant aerie, installing a fanciful vintage Murano chandelier in the shape of a giant flower in the vestibule, and enveloping the bedroom in soothing blush tones. He commissioned a woven rug with a pattern resembling scattered petals and installed wall-spanning linen curtains edged with a chevron braid, a signature touch by a designer who excels at discreet eye-pleasing details. Patrick left the terrazzo flooring in the primary bath but quietened the space with chic raffia panels that he had coated with gesso, like the rest of the walls. "My Paris apartment," the client joked to Patrick of her sanctuary above the trees.

The day after the couple spent their first night in their newly designed home, Patrick received a one-word text. It read, "Ah."

"For me, that's mission accomplished," said Patrick.

Page 58: Patrick gave the interiors a thoroughly modern makeover, beginning with the entrance foyer. The blackened window frames now tie into the original checkerboard limestone flooring and draw the eye to a striking black and white canvas.

Previous spread: By updating an existing armchair with a jazzy Pierre Frey fabric and placing distinctive artworks with room to breathe, there's now a dynamic tension between the house's traditional elements and its new contemporary attitude.

Opposite and above: While the bones of the vestibule remain the same, Patrick made soft, subtle changes, such as applying Marmorino plaster to the walls and a faux limestone finish to the jambs to make everything quieter and more refined.

Following spread: Patrick created subtle drama in the living room by introducing an ethereal color—"orchid," as his client calls it. The delicate hue envelops the spacious room, from the pale lavender velvet upholstery and the ombré plasterwork to the sumptuous hand-knotted silk rug.

TheCentury
WOLF KAHN

Patrick's ability to listen carefully and observe keenly served this project well. He discovered that these clients weren't driven by making hurried decisions, but rather by a thoughtful approach with no time limits—a rare luxury in today's fast-paced world.

Patrick chose Italian iron-framed outdoor furniture that melds with the exterior style of the house. Deep cushions make this an inviting spot to enjoy the garden.

ROLLING STONE · THE

Opposite: The living room's parquet floors were lightened to better connect with the adjoining limestone flooring, and the couple's antiques were rearranged for a simplified look.

Above: A peek into the newly refurbished conservatory.

Following spread: The conservatory's crown molding was treated with a faux limestone finish. The existing dark-bronze bas-relief was limewashed to match the frieze installed below the skylight to unify the space. A steel-base, marble-top table of Patrick's design is on sturdy castors so the couple can wheel it away when they wish to use the space as an extended dining area for the holidays.

Right: The dining room's glamorous update includes brightening the coffered ceiling, crisp linen curtains, and neoclassical-style chairs by Dessin Fournir upholstered in a shimmery silk chenille.

Following pages: A silk wallcovering gives the dining room a soigné look. Modern touches include a clean-lined wooden sideboard from Jean de Merry.

Above: Patrick conceived a cozy nook in the family room by sheathing the walls surrounding the fireplace with a blue-gray woven linen fabric and pulling up a pair of wing chairs whose swirly fabric riffs off the color scheme.

Opposite: On the other side of the family room, a comfortable swivel armchair sits atop a Tibetan hand-knotted silk rug by Stark. An antique side chair (one of a pair) is upholstered in a modern tweedy fabric by Holly Hunt.

Old world meets new in the family room where the original wood beams and doors form a backdrop to a knockout bronze table lamp by Hervé Van der Straeten from Ralph Pucci, an eye-catching contemporary photograph, luxurious alpaca curtains, and a mod ceiling pendant light crafted in blackened-steel and glass.

Above: A custom-made bar in the breakfast room was designed to look like a piece of fine furniture with high-gloss cabinetry and parchment doors that cleverly hide an icemaker. The wall behind it is made of silvered mirror.

Opposite: The breakfast room's oak table and chairs give the space the relaxed air of a garden room, as do the woven window treatments and a whimsical lantern pendant light.

Above: Reflective surfaces abound in the breakfast room, among them mirrored glass sconces by the Urban Electric Company set against a silvered mirror wall.

Opposite: An inset steel curio cabinet stores glassware. The grass cloth wallcovering shimmers thanks to its metallic background.

Following spread: The kitchen's original Provencal style was completely reimagined in soothing modern finishes. A pair of islands is crafted in stained riff-sawn oak with lava stone countertops; the stone mosaic backsplash is paired with marble trim around the windows for an elevated look; and the floors are Turkish limestone.

Above: A faux-bois finish to the vestibule's walls and millwork creates a stately atmosphere outside her office, while a modern light fixture punches up the style.

Opposite: The handsome powder room's walls are covered in a hand-painted wallpaper that's been treated with a coat of Venetian plaster. The sink is made from hand-carved soapstone, and the pendant light fixture is by Apparatus.

A masculine mood permeates his office. Patrick lined the walls with tooled leather that magnifies the exceptional modern art. He designed cast-bronze-and-walnut consoles to hold books and artifacts to complement the tooled-leather walls, and introduced a richly patterned rug by Marc Phillips that's high on personality.

NEIL LEIFER
ANNIE LEIBOVITZ
THE ROLLING STONES
ART OF BURNING MAN
ATLAS OF THE WORLD
US OPEN
NORMAN MAILER

Danielle Steel THE GIFT
PAUL HENDRICKSON
HEMINGWAY'S BOAT

Previous pages: The classical staircase leads to the upstairs bedrooms. On the landing, Patrick mixed periods and styles, pairing an antique chest with a modern abstract painting.

Opposite: A petal-shaped Murano glass light fixture, a 1stDibs find, and some fresh glossy paint herald the entrance to the primary suite.

Above: Because the sitting area in the primary suite feels like an aerie up in the trees, Patrick commissioned a Tibetan silk rug that recalls fallen cherry blossom petals underfoot. The pair of chairs are covered in violet alpaca.

The couple's bedroom is an oasis of calm, with a four-poster oak bed that's upholstered in a dreamy silk chenille, and floor-to-ceiling linen curtains that wrap cozily around the room.

Opposite: Patrick retained the terrazzo flooring in the primary bath but inserted stylish raffia panels that he coated with gesso, like the rest of the walls, to create a hushed, spa-like space.

Above: A children's bedroom was transformed into a serene guestroom fashioned in soft lilac hues.

Following pages: A hallway of mirrors leads to the upstairs family room where an eclectic wallpaper with a large-scale pattern packs a punch. An existing armchair was updated in sleek gray chenille.

Baselitz

A Grand New Attitude

POTOMAC, MARYLAND

Patrick rarely tackles individual projects in the same way. His objectives might be similar but as he is adept at working in a variety of styles, his approach remains fluid and open-minded. "As a designer, I tend to articulate a vision for each home, each space, and then hope we can move on to the specific details," Patrick said. "But sometimes it takes all of my life skills to figure out what clients want to achieve aesthetically."

Such was the case with Michael and Diane, who bought this stately mansion in Potomac, Maryland. The six-bedroom residence was styled after a French palace with ornamental flourishes. It featured high ceilings, interior arches and columns, and ornate cornices and moldings. Patrick typically spends time in the early design phase with new clients trying to learn about their taste and glean what they envision for their home. Then he conceives a design scheme and "runs with it until the grand unveiling," as he describes it. This house was different.

Michael and Diane were highly analytical, methodical, and particular but had difficulty articulating an aesthetic style. When Patrick began asking them questions, such as where they liked to travel and what kind of hotels they preferred, his clients revealed distinctly modern tastes. For example, they had vacationed at a tropical Aman resort, where they had appreciated the spare, spa-like environment. For Patrick, that was the aha moment. He had extracted their modern bent and went on to conceive a contemporary theme using a refined palette and elegant furnishings to imbue the classical bones of the house with a clean, fresh spirit. "We took what was there and elevated the look by adding modern furnishing and seductive textiles, along with glamorous flourishes," he explained.

Since 2018, Patrick has put significant effort into revitalizing the rooms, one by one, like a meticulous work in progress. Early on he handled a son's room. More recently he finished the primary suite and its sophisticated dressing room. At the time of publishing, Patrick has yet to tackle the kitchen. "I joke with them that we should just convert one of their bedrooms into a pied-à-terre for me as I will be working on this project until I'm dead," he said with a laugh.

His first order of business was to focus on the expansive living area comprising two spaces separated by a pair of columns. "What am I going to do here?" he wondered about the first space, which is located adjacent to the bar and serves as a glorified passageway to the second space—the formal living area. His invention was to create a small salon that offers extra seating near the custom-designed fluted-wood bar without disrupting the flow of the overall space. It's elegantly furnished with a serpentine double-sided sofa atop a clean-lined woven-leather rug, existing antique armchairs that Patrick reupholstered in a gilded Art Deco–inspired fabric, and demilune sideboards and sleek side tables with sculptural flair.

The light-filled formal living room is Patrick's modern interpretation of a grand Parisian salon. He anchored the space with sleek, curved armchairs upholstered in nude leather, a voluminous sofa, and a soigné daybed facing the carved fireplace. He replaced an ornate chandelier with a ribbon-like aluminum light fixture and energized a corner with an ode to black and white, pairing fun swivel chairs upholstered in a light cozy fabric with striking photographs of the Miami skyline.

Michael and Diane wanted a stylish bar for entertaining and Patrick gave them one that's as swank as any restaurant lounge. He paneled the walls with white-painted fluted wood—a modern twist on the room's ornamental moldings—and he designed a tufted banquette that sweeps around the curve of the bay window. A crystal light fixture in the shape of a large smoke ring sparkles beneath a ceiling aglow with high-gloss paint. It's a most festive and alluring space. "I have so much experience being in bars that designing them comes naturally," Patrick declared with a smile.

The primary suite got a full makeover. Patrick pared down the trim and painted the ceiling a serene high-gloss blue-gray, and then filled the room with interesting furnishings, such as a group of curvaceous seating that brings intimacy to the voluminous space. For the dressing room, which had been a warren of nooks and crannies, he stripped the ornate moldings and fancy flourishes and created a crisp white area tricked out with chic semi-translucent Poliform closet doors and marble islands.

"If we had found Patrick fifteen years ago our house would have been decorated fifteen years ago. We went through many designers before meeting him, but it never clicked. No one had all the pieces of the puzzle," Diane recalled. "Patrick's work has an elegant simplicity to it. The rooms speak to you; they have a character to them. They're beautiful, they're elegant, and yet they're warm and cozy."

Page 104: The grand salon was given a fresh, crisp look by toning down flourishes like ornamental molding with white paint and introducing modern furnishings as a counterpoint to the elaborate adornment.

Previous spread: For the swank, minimally furnished bar area, Patrick designed a curvaceous built-in banquette, painted the ceiling in an alluring high-gloss blue-gray, and added a shimmering pendant light for a festive touch.

Above and opposite: Fluted, white-painted wood, marble-clad niches, and illuminated shelving dress up the bar.

SPRINGSTEEN

Previous spread: Patrick transformed a passageway from the foyer to the formal living room into a small salon where a custom-made Vladimir Kagan–style double sofa provides a perfect perch for parties.

Left: Bold artworks above leather-covered demilune sideboards create a lovely juxtaposition of classical elements and a playful modern attitude.

Following pages: A corner in the main salon is a testament to the quiet power of decorating in black and white.

Once a dark space, the family dining room is now infused with springtime touches, among them pale Marmorino plaster walls, lavender curtains, a lilac-flecked fabric on existing chairs, and a cheery gingham-wallpapered ceiling.

Patrick's solution to creating intimacy in the voluminous primary bedroom was to pump up the scale of the furnishings, such as a lofty four-poster bed paired with a group of shapely seating. Plaster and iron light fixtures hang from a high-gloss painted ceiling, and a silk rug shimmers underfoot.

Above: A rabbit warren of walls and nooks was gutted to conceive this tailored dressing room. The space is lined with semi-reflective closets by Poliform and anchored by marble islands illuminated with bronze-and-linen drum light fixtures. Steel-and-glass doors to the right lead into the primary bath.

Opposite: Inspired by the spa-like feeling of a tropical resort, the couple's serene bath features a minimalist oval tub, hushed marble flooring, and a steel-trimmed, glass-enclosed shower.

Above and opposite: For Michael's office, a double-height space that was once dark and heavy, Patrick elevated the surroundings with a fresh take on gray—from glossy paint and a sculptural light fixture to a swirling Cole & Son wallpaper on the ceiling that echoes the existing railing.

Following spread: The basement level was completely revamped into a games room and energized with a colorful wallpaper mural.

SPORT
Ball
FEStIVAL

FULL SWING
MONDIAL

A Modern Cottage

BALTIMORE COUNTY, MARYLAND

Central to Patrick's process is a good client story that helps him understand who he's working with and envision a design scheme. This suburban Maryland home certainly has one. The homeowners were newly empty nesters and exploring the idea of downsizing to a luxury condominium tower in Baltimore from their spacious family residence in a gated community surrounding a golf course. But the wife started getting cold feet: She was uncomfortable living so high in the sky with a balconied terrace and young grandchildren underfoot.

Around the same time, the husband, who serves as chairman of the golf course, had his own worries: Mature trees on another resident's property were heavily shading an area of the golf course grass. When his request to have the trees removed failed, he bought this Cotswold-style stone cottage instead. His plan was to quickly renovate the dark, ornate interiors and flip the property while he and his wife continued to look for a suitable home. Then came Covid and their decision to not only shelter in place, but to stay there forever following an enlightening rejuvenation of the house.

What ensued was nothing short of serendipitous: A gut renovation and a thoroughly stylish and modern makeover by Patrick. His overarching vision was to transform the dated, lackluster rooms into welcoming, airy interiors with a crisp, tailored aesthetic—a departure for the couple, whose previous home was more traditional.

The Cotswold vibe of the peaked-roof stone house remains firmly planted outside the front door, where Patrick chose a jaunty blue for the exterior trim and lightened the stonework to look fresh. Inside, a pared-down aesthetic presides. Patrick wanted to evoke a bright, clean, and calming sensibility during the pandemic's period of uncertainty with an edited furniture plan that would work long afterwards. In terms of architectural adjustments, he added glass windows and French doors to the main living spaces to bring in light and views of the undulating landscape, painting their steel frames black so they visually recede. He fashioned a metal-and-glass rail that appears to float upstairs.

The furnishings throughout the house are shapely and comfortable and the fabrics are soft to the touch and to the eye. It's an expressive, soothing combination designed to elicit ease and relaxation and quietly complement the couple's radiant art collection that includes standout modern and contemporary paintings, photography, and sculpture. Acquiring those furnishings, however, required a creative approach. "It was like an episode of *Chopped* [the food competition reality show] because there was literally zero design supply during the pandemic and we had to make do with what we could find," Patrick recalled. "Our designers had to rent U-Hauls to pick up furniture at manufacturers because there was no shipping."

For the foyer, Patrick conceived a minimalist space to set the tone, furnishing the area with an eye-catching blue stainless-steel convex mirror above a mid-century modern cane-back chair and a glossy, sculptural side table. In the living room, the designer selected creamy neutral fabrics, from a subtle snakeskin-like fabric on an armchair to a textured woven linen on the voluptuous sofas. "I'm constantly trying to find peace and harmony through design," he said.

A chic breakfast nook with a glass-top table and a built-in upholstered banquette is a cheerful, light-filled spot to start the day. "I do have clever ideas once in a while," Patrick admitted with a smile. Next to the breakfast room, he created his-and-her offices for the couple to work from home. A variety of outdoor seating arrangements allow them to practically live outside in warm months, and includes a magical screened porch that serves as a plein-air living and dining area complete with a hidden widescreen TV.

The primary suite is an oasis of calm. Patrick dressed the room in luxurious light-colored fabrics, injecting just a few jewel tones, such as a gold velvet loveseat and grape-colored pillows, for a dash of glamour. He took out walls in the primary bedroom to create a private lounge-like sitting area that he padded with a three-dimensional wallcovering that evokes sculptural tiles to create a near-silent haven to recline and watch TV, read a book, or enjoy a drink. He encased the primary bathroom in hushed shades of marble and textural surfaces, including a ribbed backsplash and fluted-glass cabinetry, and installed black steel-framed windows and doors that give the spa-like space a tailored look. These are the small but visually exciting flourishes that Patrick takes pride in executing and add up to an impactful design. "These architectural elements are like little jewels that elevate the space," he said.

"Chasing details," as Patrick describes it, is a huge part of his job. "An absolute dedication to attention to detail is a founding principle of our work—to the point of unhealthy obsession," he added with a laugh.

Page 128: The exterior stone, originally in a patchwork of tans and browns, was chemically lightened to a soft gray and the trim was painted deep blue for a fresh take on Cotswold cottage style.

Above: A minimalist foyer with honed limestone flooring and a walnut-capped glass stair railing greets visitors at the entrance.

Opposite: Eye-catching touches include a mid-century–style cane-back chair, updated with a magenta velvet cushion, beneath a mesmerizing blue convex mirror.

Previous spread: Patrick conceived the family's clean-lined living room to showcase the homeowners' art collection, grouping comfortable modern seating with a sleek leather-covered cocktail table.

Above: A French Modernist–inspired armchair is covered in a snakeskin-patterned chenille, and a porcelain sculpture on a pedestal plays up the nearby artworks.

Opposite: Patrick chose this tailored sofa for its shapely silhouette and extreme comfort—"two things that don't always go together," he noted. A vintage table lamp perches on a leather-trimmed side table.

FRENCH RIVIERA
DORIE & MATT
GARRY WINOGRAND
Lorenzo Quinn
MARILYN MONROE
Andy Warhol Prints
PATRICK SUTTON
STORIED INTERIORS
CHIHULY

Simplicity rules in the dining room where crisp details include dark wood-trimmed armchairs that pick up the bronzed brass frames of Holly Hunt sconces. Patrick customized an RH dining table with a faux finish to make the base look cerused and then polished the top. The graphic handwoven wool rug is by Amadi.

17.7.70.
I

Above: In the kitchen, a custom-made cabinet mimics the steel-framed windows.

Opposite: The new kitchen is rendered in cerused walnut cabinetry, black steel accents, and creamy Taj Mahal quartzite.

"It's just fresh," declares Patrick of the breakfast nook, whose caned barrel chairs by Baker are pulled up to a sculptural glass-top table that the designer painted white. A niche holds African papier-maché vases.

Previous spread: An outdoor living room embraces nature while boasting creature comforts, among them a TV that rises out of the console at the push of a button.

Above: Opportunities to congregate alfresco abound. Modern Adirondack chairs, from Design Within Reach, surround a firepit.

Opposite: Low-slung seating with deep cushions outfit another terrace.

Patrick created an inviting shared office for his clients using spare but sublime materials: warm walnut for the built-in desks and shelving; handsome Claros Grey marble for the fireplace surround; and a shapely wood-and-marble center table.

CH RIVIERA

CHANEL

Previous spread: By opening some walls in the primary bedroom, Patrick was able to craft a more symmetrical space amid awkward angles created by the peaked roof. Now it's an ethereal oasis executed in shades of cream and gray so that the focal point is on the vibrant works of art.

Above: A cozy sitting area off the bedroom is clad in an artful three-dimensional wallcovering.

Opposite: Steel-framed, fluted-glass doors provide light and privacy in the marble-lined bathroom; the tub is by Victoria + Albert.

Singular details elevate the elegant bath, among them cerused white oak cabinetry that has a whitewashed linear look, a backsplash of fluted Calacatta marble, and a subtle chevron pattern in the marble wall tiles.

A Temple of Wellness

LUTHERVILLE, MARYLAND

Every homeowner has a dream. For one Maryland couple who work in the fitness industry, their dream was to have a guesthouse where they could share all the elements of good health and well-being with their family and friends. They envisioned tranquil living areas and bedrooms that promoted serenity; a full gym with all its accoutrements, including a massage room and spa; lounges to gather and play games; and an inviting pool cabana to celebrate outdoor living. A master interpreter of fantasies, Patrick knew exactly how to translate this couple's vision into reality—especially since he had worked on multiple projects with them in the past. "By the time we were designing this house, I knew their interests intuitively," he said.

They wanted the guesthouse to feel like it was rooted to the surrounding woodland and nestled into the undulating landscape of the Maryland countryside. The architecture, which was handled by Tom Kligerman, founder of the New York firm Kligerman Architecture & Design, features earthy materials. Natural wood shingles for the exterior were stained a chocolate brown to emulate tree bark and local stones for retaining walls and pathways give the property a sense of timelessness. "There is a muscular quality to the winding stone-wall steps leading up to the property," Patrick explained. "We wanted that feeling like you are meandering through a mountain pass for a little bit of romance."

The heart of the two-bedroom house is a double-height living and dining area flooded with natural light through huge picture windows and clerestory windows and anchored by a bluestone fireplace built into a shiplap-clad wall. "In spite of its volume, the area is both intimate and grand, cozy but voluminous," Kligerman said.

Because Patrick knows that interiors tell stories of their own, he conceived serene, welcoming rooms using light colors and subtle finishes to evoke a sense of calm and well-being. And he selected eclectic furnishings and objects, mixing periods and styles, "so that everything isn't new like a showroom," he said. He found a pair of decorative antique Chinese wood panels that were hung above the living area's interior doorways and displayed graphic black-and-white photographs above the fireplace for visual punch. "The mix of antiquities and modern photography is a nice juxtaposition," he noted.

Other lovely juxtapositions happened when Patrick placed a rustic hand-carved armoire from Mexico against the interior's crisp white walls and paired a vintage Asian buffet with the dining area's sleek walnut table. Knowing that the homeowner owned an equestrian estate, Patrick subtly referenced the equestrian world by employing stitched leather and bronze bridle shapes in the custom-made light fixture above the dining table.

The vast gym pavilion is a temple of health whose vaulted design was conceived with an industrial spirit for this athletic family. The walls are clad in board-formed concrete beneath a soaring steel-webbed ceiling paneled in walnut.

"Everything we did was in collaboration with Patrick," noted Kligerman, who met the designer while on a bus in Copenhagen during a design conference and was later introduced by Patrick to the Maryland couple. "The moral of the story is be nice to everybody you meet," Kligerman recalled with a laugh. "Patrick is smart, he's funny, and he's thoughtful," the architect added. "His in-depth knowledge was helpful not just to the process but to the overall aesthetic. New collaborations like this are what make our work interesting."

ART HOUSE

Opposite: In the light-filled living and dining room, antique Chinese wood panels hang above a pair of doorways, the fireplace surround is made of Tundra gray marble, and a graphic diptych photograph is displayed against white-painted shiplap.

Above and following spread: A neutral palette serves as a quiet canvas, drawing the eye to the verdant wooded landscape. The space is energized with some arresting details, including a hand-carved Mexican cabinet and a vibrantly patterned Moroccan rug.

ART HOUSE

The furnishings in the dining area are rustic yet refined, among them an antique Asian chest, woven leather director's chairs, and a custom-made leather-and-brass light fixture by Lucca Antiques that nods to the homeowners' interest in the equestrian world.

In the kitchen, walnut cabinetry is paired with Tundra gray marble countertops, and the bronze pendant lights are by Holly Hunt. The floors throughout this level are European oak.

Patrick used a variety of soft textures and subtle hues to create a restful sensibility in a guest bedroom. The horsehair wallcovering is by Phillip Jeffries and the horn-base table lamps, sustainably sourced from South Africa, are crafted with horns shed from the animals.

A guest bathroom is all clean lines, as are the austere shiplap walls flanking a staircase down to the gym pavilion.

CYBEX
AIRRUNNER

In the gym, architect Tom Kligerman sheathed the walls in board-formed concrete beneath vaulted webbed-steel arches; the ceiling is paneled in walnut that warms up the cathedral-like space.

ATLAS OF THE WORLD
TWENTY FIFTH EDITION

Previous spread: A suite of rooms is devoted to wellness, including a lounge area outfitted with plush seating upholstered in muted tones.

Above: Patrick conceived a massage room excelling in soothing, uplifting textures. He used a shimmering beaded wallcovering by Maya Romanoff for the trayed ceiling, and sheathed the walls in a three-dimensional wallcovering by Phillip Jeffries that resembles organic handmade paper. A backlit onyx panel provides a gentle glow.

Opposite: An antique barber's chair, reupholstered in chocolate-colored leather, takes center stage in the home salon.

Left and above: A laidback Moroccan vibe suffuses the covered pool cabana thanks to rattan-and-rice-paper pendant lights and ottomans covered in a jazzy tribal print. The custom coffee table is made out of reclaimed barn timber.

Following spread: Stonework with a muscular heft surrounds the pool area, as if rooting the first floor to the earth. The wood shingles above were stained chocolate brown to match the bark of the surrounding trees.

A Mountain Retreat

JACKSON HOLE, WYOMING

The American West is endowed with majestic mountain peaks, serpentine rivers that snake through the lower valleys, and vast meadowlands where horses and cattle graze, as do an astonishing array of wildlife. Wyoming, in the northern Rocky Mountains, is the least populated state in the nation, and Jackson Hole is the heart and soul of this breathtakingly scenic region, long attracting second homeowners in search of an idyllic summer retreat.

Several years ago a couple from Maryland bought this two-story house in a luxury golf course community on the outskirts of Jackson Hole. The residence had classic Wyoming touches, such as peaked cedar-shingled rooflines, a rustic stone and wood exterior, and reclaimed wood beams and trim inside. The couple reached out to Patrick to upgrade the finishes and transform the "nice but ho-hum interiors," as Patrick described it, to put their own lively imprint on it.

The first order of business for Patrick was to listen carefully to the couple's desires and create spaces that appealed to both of their sensibilities. "They had just completed a new shingle-style house in Maryland that was quite traditional. During the course of discovery with them, it started occurring to me that they wanted something more modern for this home," Patrick recalled. "She loves antiques, objects with character, and unique lighting, while he likes modern design all the way. For each project I need to understand who we are designing for, and that comes from listening."

Patrick synthesized their tastes and established a modern yet eclectic mood in the decor. He placed an eye-catching handcrafted console with a wooden zigzag facade in the entry, above which a spherical LED lighting fixture ringed with quartz crystals is one of the many standout light fixtures deployed throughout the home. For the double-height great room beyond, he chose a spacious Italian sectional sofa upholstered in a smart gray basket weave fabric; its backless portions keep the mountain views in sight. Gauzy curtains, designed to soften the angular room, "dance in the breeze," Patrick said. He swapped out the more typical wood railings for transparent glass along the edge of the mezzanine, and installed a panel of veined smoked onyx that evokes mountain ranges between cabinetry in the dining area.

The den is the family's hangout space, so he gave it a more casual, youthful spin, decorating the room with deep, low-slung sofas upholstered in a cozy bouclé. He also combined a myriad of patterns for a layered look, including a playful geometric print for the curtains, a scribble pattern for the armchair, and pillows covered in mix-and-match antique fabrics. "Those antique pillows speak to her sensibilities, while the modern lines of the sofa speak to his. It's fun to create a space with a playful attitude that's a little less serious," Patrick said. Additional hangout spaces include a variety of stylishly furnished outdoor seating areas where the family can enjoy and celebrate the spectacular beauty of the Jackson Hole landscape.

Patrick enveloped the couple's bedroom with cocooning materials to create the feeling of a sanctuary. He covered the ceiling with seagrass and lined the walls with a natural husk fiber, "like it could be made out of something growing in the forest," he said. Soft alpaca wool curtains filter the strong high-mountain sunlight. An antique Chinese painted chest and a large carved-wood cabinet are striking components in the otherwise muted room. "I actually have the same cabinet in my bedroom," he noted. "I love the sophisticated yet somehow primitive carving. It has great texture to it."

The one area that Patrick initially wasn't quite sure how to handle—and he is not alone in this particular quandary—was the open landing at the top of the stairs created by the double-height design. "I always scratch my head and wonder, what am I going to do up there?" When Patrick realized that the husband didn't have an office in the house, he found his answer. He sheathed the area with steel-framed glass panels, hung sheer drapes for privacy, and outfitted it with unique pieces including a coffee table molded from a tree trunk, a handsome Tuareg rug with a bold pattern that recalls Native American markings, and a bronze sculpture of Crazy Horse by the Western artist John Coleman.

This space is now as purposeful as it is elegant and inviting, just like the rest of the artfully conceived house, which feels both fresh and timeless and thoroughly right for its dramatic setting. "I'm constantly trying to find peace and harmony through interior design, creating an environment to have a beautiful day," Patrick said.

Amid dark wood floors and rustic beams, Patrick injected modern touches, such as glass stair railings and intriguing light fixtures. A modular sofa configured with some backless sections provides optimal views of Wyoming's Grand Teton.

Opposite: Layers and textures are at the heart of Patrick's design for the house. In the entry he paired a vivid painting by Hunt Slonem with a hand-carved credenza and an onyx trough, both made by Mexican artisans.

Above: The high volume of the entry was ideal for hanging a unique spherical pendant studded with quartz crystals.

Marlboro
Folk-Lore
AMERICAN

Left: In the double-height great room, the walls were treated with textural Marmorino plaster to give the soaring space some warmth and character, while large-scale artworks depicting wildlife add visual panache.

Following spread: In contrast to the light-filled great room, the nearby family room has a cozy vibe thanks to punchy fabrics and a moody palette. The curtains feature a tribal-like pattern, a swivel lounge chair is upholstered in a graphic woven fabric, and a jolt of deep blue comes from a chunky Moroccan rug by Marc Phillips. The Native American pottery was sourced in Jackson Hole.

Elements in the kitchen and dining area nod to the natural world, from a wall of gray smoke onyx whose pattern recalls a mountain range to the pendant light's glass drops that sparkle like the pond outside. Patrick paired a walnut dining table with rope-back armchairs upholstered in a lavender woven linen.

Previous spread and above: An outdoor sofa and chairs by Bernhardt with deep cushions are "oversized and comfortable—perfect for mountain living," according to Patrick.

Following spread: The house beautifully melds rustic materials and mountain architecture with sumptuous, up-to-the-minute furnishings indoors and out.

Page 203: The media room is another inviting space, outfitted with a wallcovering that looks like birch trees, botanical-print drapes, and a coffee table crafted with a hand-forged iron base and wood plank top.

“She loves antiques, objects with character, and unique lighting, while he likes modern design all the way. For each project I need to understand who we are designing for, and that comes from listening.”

Previous spread and above: In the ethereal primary bedroom, Patrick deployed colors of the landscape, such as an earthy brown in the stripes of alpaca curtains and a Mexican armoire, and shades of sand in the husk wallcovering on the ceiling and walls.

Left: Leather-trimmed brass sconces by Ralph Lauren for Visual Comfort flank a scalloped walnut headboard.

Above: For Patrick, small details pack a punch. He adorned the primary bathroom's linen curtains with a leather-appliquéd wool trim. *Opposite:* Contemporary artwork enlivens the serene space.

N°5
CHANEL
PARIS
EAU DE PARFUM

Marlboro
Folk-Lore

Left: An awkward loft space was transformed into the husband's office by way of steel-paneled glass walls that are shielded with curtains for privacy. The Moroccan-style runner by Marc Phillips complements the American West adornments.

Above: In his office, the bronze sculpture of Crazy Horse is by the Western artist John Coleman, and the Tuareg rug is by Amadi.

Opposite: Handsome accents include a walnut desk paired with a leather-covered chair, and a shapely wooden armchair upholstered in a textured bouclé.

Page 214: A Western spirit inhabits a guestroom lined with a rustic husk wallcovering.

Page 215: An existing bedroom was transformed into a fashionable bunkroom, complete with shiplap details and cheerful fabrics for the curtains and carpeting.

Above and opposite: Reclaimed wood was used for a wall in another bedroom, where terracotta-hued curtains, a cowhide-topped wood desk, and a leather swivel chair epitomize a fresh take on mountain style.

La Dolce Vita

REHOBOTH BEACH, DELAWARE

When an interior designer and client share near identical tastes, the stars almost certainly align. The process is often seamless and the results magical. That was case for this oceanfront house in Delaware. Patrick had conceived the interiors of a new three-bedroom home in Annapolis for a tech developer in the e-commerce industry. They had hit it off from the very first meeting when Patrick brought along the latest look book of men's clothing from luxury fashion designer Brunello Cucinelli as inspiration for the palette. It turned out that they both admired the Italian designer's exquisite fabrics and detailing, and they had the same passion for fine Swiss watches and British cars. "We just got along very well," Patrick recalled.

In 2020, the client, Chip, acquired a very special property in the dunes of Rehoboth Beach, Delaware, and once again turned to his trusted interior designer and kindred spirit. The original mansion, known as Shell House, had been built in 1920 by a member of the du Pont family, the celebrated American industrialists. The house had seven bedrooms and bathrooms and offered rare birds-eye views of the Atlantic Ocean to the east and tranquil Silver Lake to the west. But it had fallen into severe disrepair.

In its place, Chip wanted a bespoke beachfront mansion that he could share with his tightknit family of six siblings and his many nieces and nephews. He tasked the design team, which included Kimmel Studio Architects, to create a home with a timeless, classic look. "I wanted this house to feel like it had been here forever," Chip said.

Patrick's designs are always constructed around narratives, and this new 18,500-square-foot residence has many stories to divulge. An early concept focused on the overall mood the designer and homeowner sought to convey throughout the house. Chip wanted open spaces that drew his family together, not dispersed them apart. There are almost no doors in the living areas, and he rejected the idea of a screen porch, for being too separate and closed, in favor of a breezy oceanfront veranda.

He embraced Patrick's scheme for a bright, white, wide-open living and dining area that faces the beach and exudes a chic summery feeling. The low-slung furniture in sand-colored fabrics helps keep the focus on the view. The lighting became an opportunity for Patrick to introduce some sculptural exuberance to the ceiling. Illuminated alabaster rings that recall clouds float above the dining table; a chandelier crafted with waves of dangling glass beads resembles a school of fish swimming above the piano.

The spacious area includes an open entertaining kitchen, behind which a door leads to a full working kitchen painted in high-gloss blue, Chip's favorite color. Patrick inserted a snappy cedar trim to drawers and cabinets, much like Brunello Cucinelli might tailor a cashmere sweater with suede. Behind one cabinet is what Patrick calls a James Bond bar—a secret drinks cupboard lined in rosewood and rainbow onyx.

For the street side of the house, which overlooks a pristine lake, Patrick conjured an into-the-woods setting. He created a cozy lakeside lounge with cedar-clad walls, rustic limestone floors, and a big stone fireplace that's "perfect for rainy weather or a cool fall day. Everyone can read, hang out, and play games," Patrick explained.

When Chip mentioned that he wanted to lean into his Italian heritage—he comes from a large Italian–Irish family—Patrick suggested they travel to Italy to source the marble. They had a field day in a Tuscan mountain quarry where they selected nearly three dozen different types of stone, among them a dazzling blue quartzite deployed on the walls of the open kitchen and in Chip's bathroom.

Rummaging through Florence's finest antiques shops, they snapped up a pair of mid-century travertine lamps for the library. In Milan they plucked a walnut cocktail table by Armani Casa off the showroom floor. Patrick adorned one bedroom with vintage photographs of the Amalfi coast that evoke Italian-style summer splendor.

The new house features nine bedrooms, beginning with a souped-up bunk room on the garden level with teak walls and full beds—"perfect for young children or inebriated adults," Patrick joked. A sculptural staircase lyrically spirals up through the center of the house, culminating in a conservatory-style skylight that spreads light throughout the house. Each bedroom on the upper floor has a unique personality and subtle, superlative details, yet they share a relaxing spa-like quality.

For the primary bedroom, Patrick paired cerused walnut millwork with upholstered wall panels in a nuanced, patterned fabric trimmed in leather for a tailored look, and he fashioned an inviting sofa banquette into the curves of a glass-walled turret. "With sweeping ocean views, every bedroom feels like a stateroom on a ship, yet none of the spaces feels grand—they are all comfortable," Patrick said. "I didn't want this to be the standard blue-and-white beach house. We really wanted something more soothing and thoughtful."

DOLCE VITA

Page 218: In the entry of this new beach house, a sculptural staircase crafted in plaster recalls a nautilus shell. A custom-made steel bench and a marble center table amplify the sinuous curves.

Pages 222–23: Inspired by early-twentieth-century manses built along the Eastern seaboard, this new shingle-style house is situated in the dunes of Rehoboth Beach, a popular resort town in Delaware.

Previous spread: The covered porch was conceived as a gathering space for family and friends, and features low-slung furnishings that keep the focus on the spectacular ocean views.

Left: Patrick deployed fabrics in light-colored hues throughout the open living area to give the space an airy, relaxed feeling.

Above: High ceilings gave Patrick the opportunity to hang visually intriguing lighting such as the alabaster fixture above the dining table that resembles floating clouds. The marble sculpture at the far end is by artist Richard Erdman.

Following page: In the living area's turreted nook, a glass-bead chandelier above the piano recalls a school of fish.

The lighting became an opportunity for Patrick to introduce some sculptural exuberance to the ceiling. A chandelier crafted with waves of dangling glass beads resembles a school of fish swimming above the piano.

SLIM AARONS
DOLCE VITA

Left: The fireplace surround is crafted from Vermont crystal stratus that picks up the hues of the furniture fabrics. The punchy silkscreen print of poppies is by Donald Sultan.

Top: The marble sculpture is by artist Richard Erdman.

The entertaining kitchen includes a large island that can accommodate many guests at breakfast and lunch. The wall behind it is lined with blue quartzite, one of the many stones Patrick and Chip sourced from an Italian quarry. Patrick tricked out the La Cornue range and cabinetry with polished and brushed steel trim. The wall of crystal stratus recalls a Japanese etching of a turbulent sea.

A door behind the white kitchen area leads to a spacious, full working kitchen rendered in high-gloss blue, the homeowner's favorite color. Nickel and linen drum-shaped pendant lights illuminate the room, and a vintage photograph by Henri Cartier-Bresson of a child carrying wine bottles injects joie de vivre.

Above: Patrick created a secret bar behind the kitchen cabinetry's pocket doors, lining it with rosewood and rainbow onyx.

Opposite: Details abound, from the fish scale–shaped Moroccan tiles that line the walls to the cedar-trimmed cabinetry that visually connects with the adjacent cedar-paneled lounge.

Above: A sculptural central staircase, crafted in plaster with a walnut handrail, brings guests from the garden-level entry to the main living floor.

Opposite: Upon arriving, the first room revealed is the library, where artful furnishings include custom-designed travertine-wrapped end tables to match the mid-century table lamps Patrick discovered in Italy.

FLORENCE
THE PAINTINGS & FRESCOES
The New York Times
THE COMPLETE FRONT PAGES

Because the owner wanted to encourage his nephews and nieces to read, Patrick created an inviting library lined with wall-to-wall-bookshelves and tailored seating covered in soft, comfortable fabrics. The coffee table is by Armani Casa, and the large-scale photograph by Massimo Listri depicts a Venetian palazzo.

UNDAUNTED
TUSCANY
WINE
SLIM AARONS
ANCIENT EGYPT

THE WORLD ATLAS OF WINE
Cartier
PANTHÈRE
West

Page 242: In a nearby powder room, patterns are at play with textural Venetian plaster walls and a custom-designed rainbow onyx vanity. An octagonal mirror is inset into the backsplash.

Page 243: The lakeside lounge has an earthy vibe—ideal for playing cards and doing puzzles on a rainy day. The mahogany-and-leather director's chairs are by Armani Casa.

Above: Patrick developed a moodier palette for this part of the house, cladding the walls in clear red cedar.

Opposite: The circular pendant light is made of bronze, and the fireplace is of the same rubble stone as the exterior.

Following spread: The back of the house faces the garden and lake beyond.

Left: The covered porch overlooking the garden features a Chippendale-style lattice design for the window-like side screens and exterior railings, along with cedar shake walls and wood decking.

Following page: Patrick transformed a turret into a cozy seating area in the primary bedroom. A custom-made banquette is lined with walnut, and floor-to-ceiling curtains can close off the space from the rest of the room.

"With sweeping ocean views, every bedroom feels like a stateroom on a ship, yet none of the spaces feels grand—they are all comfortable."

Right: Patrick chose finishes that would create a relaxed, beachside feeling, such as cerused-walnut wall and window trim, and a ceiling made from tea-stained Marmorino plaster.

Following pages: Chip's love of men's tailoring led Patrick to design upholstered wall panels trimmed in hand-stitched suede. The dressing room walls are clad in cerused walnut, and the fluting above the cabinets carries into the primary bathroom, where fluted walnut was also used for the vanity.

The primary bathroom evokes the allure of the sea. The walls are lined with contrasting slabs of blue quartzite and Calacatta Michelangelo marble, all hand selected from an Italian quarry.

For an oceanfront guestroom, Patrick designed a cozy reading area in a window bay and swathed the space in multiple textures of blue and cream. The artwork above the daybed is by Alexander Calder, and the vintage leather-paneled dresser was bought in Florence.

In another bedroom, Patrick took advantage of a charming little nook to outfit it with a daybed enclosed with curtains—an ideal arrangement for family members with small children. Beachy touches include raffia-lined walls and a limestone-clad shower.

Opposite: The top floor, tucked into the eaves of the roof, houses two bedrooms. This one features geometric-patterned wallpaper that offers more visual interest than had Patrick just used white paint. The artwork is by Alexander Calder.

Above: One of the many private terraces throughout the house.

Page 264: The bathroom of another top-floor bedroom has a shower outfitted with ribbed terrazzo tilework, fluted walnut vanities, and buff-colored plaster walls.

Page 265: A simple graphic wallcovering creates a soothing atmosphere in the bedroom, which overlooks the lake. The black-and-white photograph is by George Hoyningen-Huene.

SLIM AARONS · LA DOLCE VITA

Opposite: A bedroom suite is large enough for a desk area. Patrick decorated the room with a blue-gray raffia wallcovering, sandy beige rug, and an evocative photograph of the Italian coast.

Above: A hand-carved wood cabinet hides a television in another guest bedroom.

An area on the top floor was conceived as a late-night salon to play billiards and shuffleboard. Patrick designed a banquette with cream-colored leather upholstery that picks up hues in the bar area's honey onyx walls. Handsome touches include timber beams, rustic plaster, and plaid carpeting.

Above: A home office occupies the top-floor turret, providing breathtaking views. Patrick added billowing wraparound curtains to soften the space and block sun when needed, while a glass and aluminum pendant fixture reflects light. The bronze is by Frederic Remington.

Opposite: The architect conceived an artful conservatory-style skylight that brightens all four floors of the house.

Following spread: Recalling a nautilus shell, the spiral staircase winds through the core of the house. The wide-plank white oak flooring is covered with a heathery wool runner that evokes beach sand and prevents slipping.

For the garden-level media room, Patrick opted for clean-lined, super comfortable furnishings, including upholstered swivel armchairs and deep sofas. He added custom woven-leather inserts to Holly Hunt ottomans inset with walnut. The steel-framed windows and doors are lined with teak.

Page 276: Because the lower level is partially subterranean, Patrick kept the palette earthy, cladding walls in Dominican coral stone and the floors with Turkish limestone. The twentieth-century painting is by André Hambourg.

Page 277 and above: A nautical spirit pervades this elegant bunkroom, thanks to glossy blue and white paints, teak-colored raffia walls, and a zingy graphic rug. Yacht pulls at the base of each bunk reveal trundle beds so up to ten people can sleep here.

Opposite: The wine room was conceived to be like a bodega, where the homeowner and his guests can venture to choose wines arranged by region for dinner. The jewel-box space is crafted in walnut with brass inlays. Gilded toasted cork panels inset into the shelves add shimmer, as does the sliding brass ladder.

Above: Teak fins were inserted in the ground-floor hallways to create a subtle visual division between spaces; here, for example, screening the bowling alley beyond.

Right: A massive 10-foot-tall and 4-foot-wide door at the entrance, painted royal blue, greets guests, who can store their shoes in a custom-built teak console. Overhead, a faux laylight is embellished with a Celtic motif in steel that pays homage to the owner's Irish heritage.

Company Profile

At Patrick Sutton, we believe each home we live in, each space we occupy, each room that holds us, tells a story of who we are and what we aspire to be. We approach each of our projects as a story waiting to be told; a specific tale of the dreams and aspirations of our client coupled with the unique spirit of the place they have chosen as home. Through empathic listening and with a thorough understanding of the confluence of place and objectives, we develop a narrative specific to each client and their locale. This allows us to craft a design that is consistent in vision and reinforced down to the smallest detail.

The results are authentic spaces that reflect our clients rather than us. They are homes and interiors that speak to a diversity of ideas rather than a preordained aesthetic, and ultimately a body of work whose common thread is the depth of vision given to us by the people for whom we design. The stories are theirs; our job is to tell them using skills honed from a lifetime of travel, clarity of vision, and commitment to excellence.

It takes many hands to build great things, and I am fortunate to have shared my studio with talented and dedicated team members. These individuals are the behind-the-scenes heroes who make our projects come together.

Mary Carballo
Stacy Prather Connelly
Genevieve Cox
Mary Dunn
Ashley Hare
Cecilia Hutt
Ira Imerlishvili
Jeff Langston
Nicholas Meeks
Antonia Miller
Casey Moers
Debra Potter
Robert Unger
Emily Ward
Ethan Weiss-Starr

Acknowledgments

This book and the work depicted within it would not be possible without the trust, vision, and effort of a vast team.

First and foremost, thank you to my clients, without whom these works would not exist. It is an honor to be entrusted with their dreams and help them become reality and I am humbled to have been given the opportunity to do so.

Designs like these are only possible when working with like-minded professionals, eager to collaborate in the pursuit of excellence. I am grateful to have worked with some of the best architects, landscape architects, lighting designers, building contractors, artisans, workrooms, and craftspeople in the business. Behind each detail in every space, there were many hands ensuring their success.

Thank you to the exacting eye of photographer Richard Powers, whose powerful images fill these pages. And to stylist Anita Sarsidi, who knows precisely where to place those perfect touches to showcase our rooms in their best light.

Thank you to our intrepid author and publishing partners whose professionalism is unparalleled. To Vicky Lowry, our writer, who dived deep into the story behind the work, interviewing our clients and architects, to take us on the journey with her seemingly effortless eloquence and insight. To our designer, Nicole Boehringer, who always just gets it right. You make these books a joy to create. And to our editor, Rebecca Gross, who kept us within the guardrails and respectful of the English language.

Thank you to *VERANDA* editor in chief, Steele Marcoux, who took time from her incredibly busy day job to write the most perfect Foreword I could ask for. And to Chesie Breen and the team at NivenBreen for their sage advice and help getting the word out.

Of course, to my incredible team at Patrick Sutton Interior Design, who share the common passion to create meaningful, lasting work and the desire for our clients to enjoy the process every day.

A special shout out to Genny Cox, my right hand on this book as well as the last. Always organized, insightful, and beloved by everyone who works with her, Genny is the glue that holds it all together.

Lastly, to my sons, Cooper and Cole, and my beautiful and brilliant wife, Tracy, thank you for your unswerving love and support, always given with a smile and words of encouragement. When the world seemingly seeks to impart its weight on my shoulders, you are always there to remind me of what matters most and lift the unnecessary burdens.

Project Credits

A Passion for Design, pp 12–57

Location: Washington, D.C.
Architect: Thomson & Cooke Architects
Landscape Architect: Campion Hruby Landscape Architects
General Contractor: Pyramid Builders
Lighting Designer: Orsman Design
Photographers: David Burroughs, pp 36–37; Richard Powers, pp 12, 16–35, 38–57
Stylist: Anita Sarsidi

A Breath of Fresh Air, pp 58–103

Location: Washington, D.C.
General Contractor: Pyramid Builders
Lighting Designer: Renfro Design Group
Photographer: Richard Powers
Stylist: Anita Sarsidi

A Grand New Attitude, pp 104–127

Location: Potomac, Maryland
General Contractor: Pyramid Builders
Photographer: Richard Powers
Stylist: Anita Sarsidi

A Modern Cottage, pp 128–155

Location: Baltimore County, Maryland
Architect: Levin/Brown Architects
General Contractor: J Paul Builders
Photographer: Richard Powers
Stylist: Anita Sarsidi

A Temple of Wellness, pp 156–181

Location: Lutherville, Maryland
Architect: Kligerman Architecture & Design
Landscape Architect: Hollander Design Landscape Architects
General Contractor: Pyramid Builders
Photographer: Richard Powers
Stylist: Anita Sarsidi

A Mountain Retreat, pp 182–217

Location: Jackson Hole, Wyoming
General Contractor: Jackson Contractors LLC
Photographer: Richard Powers
Stylist: Anita Sarsidi

La Dolce Vita, pp 218–281

Location: Rehoboth Beach, Delaware
Architect: Kimmel Studio Architects
Landscape Architect: Campion Hruby Landscape Architects
General Contractor: Horizon Builders
Lighting Designer: Orsman Design
Photographer: Richard Powers
Stylist: Anita Sarsidi

Published in Australia in 2025 by
The Images Publishing Group Pty Ltd
ABN 89 059 734 431

Offices

MELBOURNE
Waterman Business Centre
Suite 64, Level 2 UL40
1341 Dandenong Road
Chadstone, Victoria 3148
Australia
Tel: +61 3 8564 8122

NEW YORK
6 West 18th Street 4B
New York, NY 10011
United States
Tel: +1 212 645 1111

SHANGHAI
6F, Building C, 838 Guangji Road
Hongkou District, Shanghai 200434
China
Tel: +86 021 31260822

books@imagespublishing.com
www.imagespublishing.com

The Images Publishing Group Reference Number: IM1724

All photography is attributed in the Project Credits on pages 286–87, unless otherwise noted.
Front cover and page 2: Richard Powers (La Dolce Vita); back cover: Richard Powers (A Passion for Design);
endpapers, pages 4, 8, 282: Lauren Daue.

A catalogue record for this book is available from the National Library of Australia

Title: Tailored Interiors: The Bespoke Designs of Patrick Sutton
Author: Patrick Sutton, Vicky Lowry
ISBN: 9781864709940

This title was commissioned in IMAGES' Melbourne office and produced as follows:
Creative Direction Nicole Boehringer; *Editorial* Rebecca Gross, Jeanette Wall; *Proofing* Holly Alexander, Helen Koehne;
Production Simon Walsh, Heather Johnson

EU GPSR Authorised Representative: Easy Access System Europe Oü
Company Registration ID: 16879218 | Address: Mustamäe tee 50, 10621 Tallinn, Estonia
Email: gpsr@easproject.com | Tel: +358 40 500 3575

Printed on 157gsm Chinese Huaxia Sun matt art paper (FSC®) in China by C&C Offset Printing Co., Ltd.

IMAGES has included on its website a page for special notices in relation to this and its other publications.
Please visit www.imagespublishing.com